"WHEN WE DENY OUR STORIES, THEY DEFINE US. WHEN WE OWN OUR STORIES, WE GET TO WRITE A BRAVE NEW ENDING."

~ BRENÉ BROWN

**TO ALL WRITERS:
AUTHORS, JOURNALISTS, COPYWRITERS, PLAYWRIGHTS, SCREENWRITERS, AND CREATIVES WHO SHARE THEIR ART AND THOUGHTS SO GENEROUSLY, IMPACTING OUR LIVES SO PROFOUNDLY. THANK YOU.**

Published by LHC Publishing 2020

My Auntie Is A Writer
Text Copyright © 2020 Y. Eevi Jones
Illustrations Copyright © 2020 Y. Eevi Jones

Printed in the USA.
All rights reserved.
No part of this book may be reproduced in any form
without the written permission of the copyright holder.

All inquiries should be directed to
www.LHCpublishing.com

ISBN-13: 978-1-952517-96-9 Paperback
ISBN-13: 978-1-952517-97-6 Hardcover

CHANGEMAKERS

MY AUNTIE IS A WRITER

The Power of Written Words

written by
Eevi Jones

With pen and scratch pad in her hands,
note-taking here and there.
Aunt Julie writes down all she sees,
spotting potential everywhere.

Potential for a story,
potential for a book.
Potential for a plot and twist
that's written with a hook.

There's a whole world inside Aunt Julie.
A creation of her own.
A world awaiting to be told and shared.
Impatient to be known.

Creating mind maps, plots, and twists, storylines galore.
Keeping readers reading. Intrigued.
Yearning for more.

Her imagination's spinning
thick webs of dialogues.
New heroes and new stories,
all born within her thoughts.

She dives into deep research mode
so she can recreate
plotlines that seem real
in a world to which we can relate.

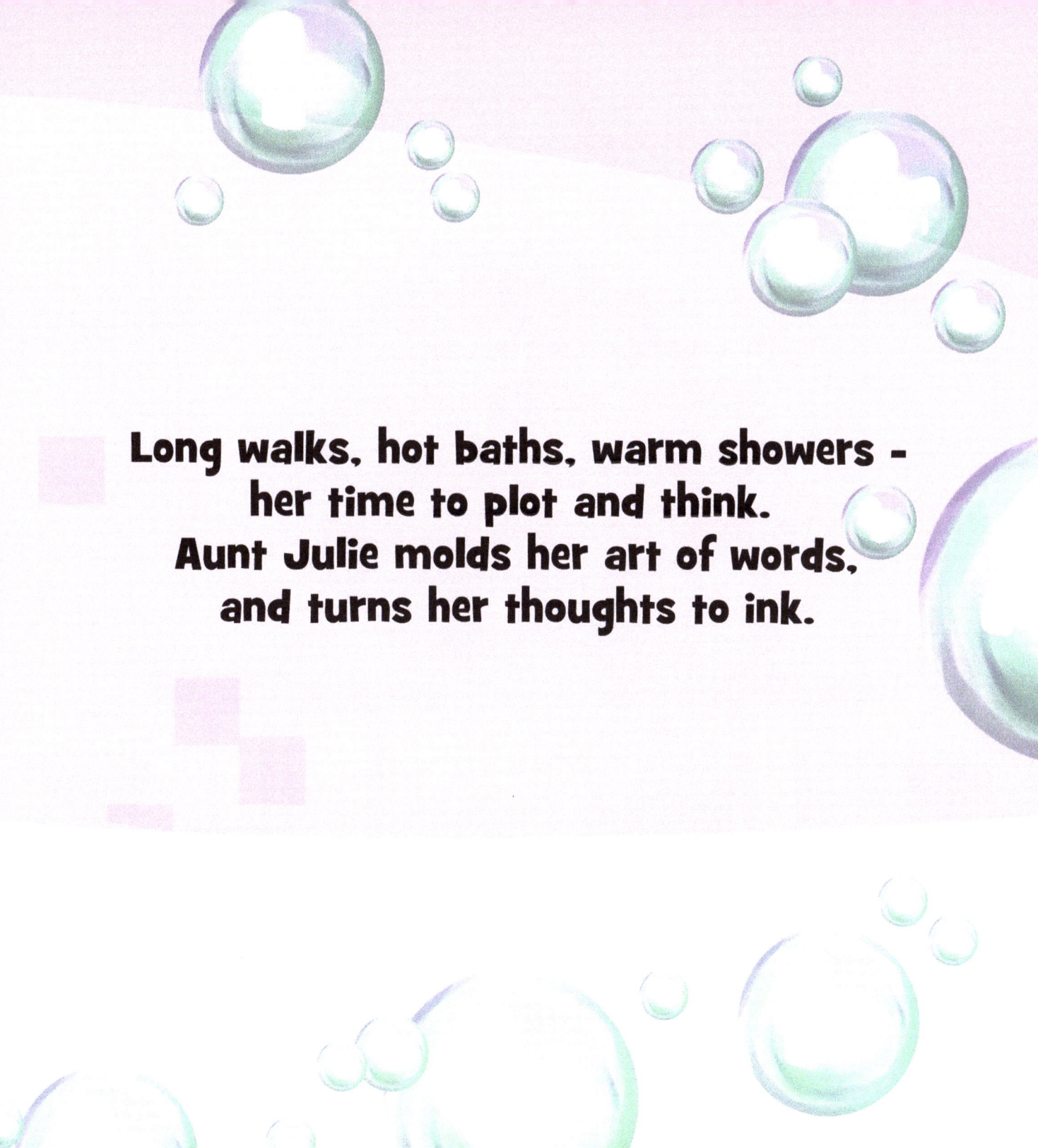

Long walks, hot baths, warm showers -
her time to plot and think.
Aunt Julie molds her art of words,
and turns her thoughts to ink.

Her creativity comes knocking,
when she's lounging in a chair,
sips coffee at a coffee shop.
Her muse strikes everywhere.

Ideas flowing from her head,
through fingers, onto page.
For writing is a process,
each step a different stage.

She writes and she erases,
then types and writes some more.
Aunt Julie scribbles notes and drafts
of angles to explore.

Writing heroes into being.
Fairies, friends, and thieves.
She names them and assigns a role.
Drafts whole identities.

Conflict, fiction, mystery,
with a sprinkle of intrigue.
Aunt Julie weaves her stories,
all gripping and unique.

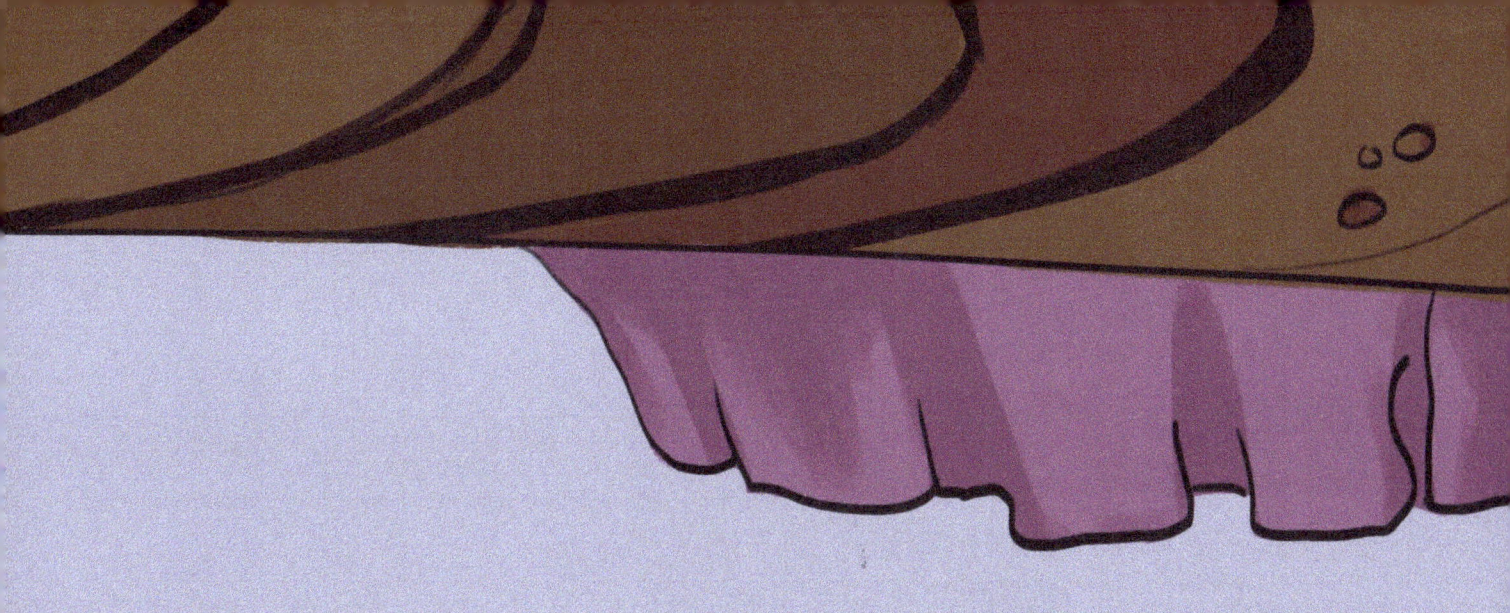

Aunt Julie captures what is hidden,
exposes the unexposed
with the creation of her string of words,
her stories, and her prose.

Her stories weaving bridges,
leading to lands heretofore unseen.
Whole worlds, so very wondrous,
to which before we've never been.

Her truth, her thoughts, her self -
Aunt Julie shares each day.
Connecting through her words
with readers a thousand miles away.

There's a reason we love stories,
where heroes grow and overcome all fear.
Because those help discover values
that we ourselves hold near and dear.

Her words that share so willingly
her weaknesses and flaws,
allow us to accept and own
those failings that are ours.

Her words are like a blazing torch,
shining a light so bright and strong
into corners of our shadows
to reveal all that has been there all along.

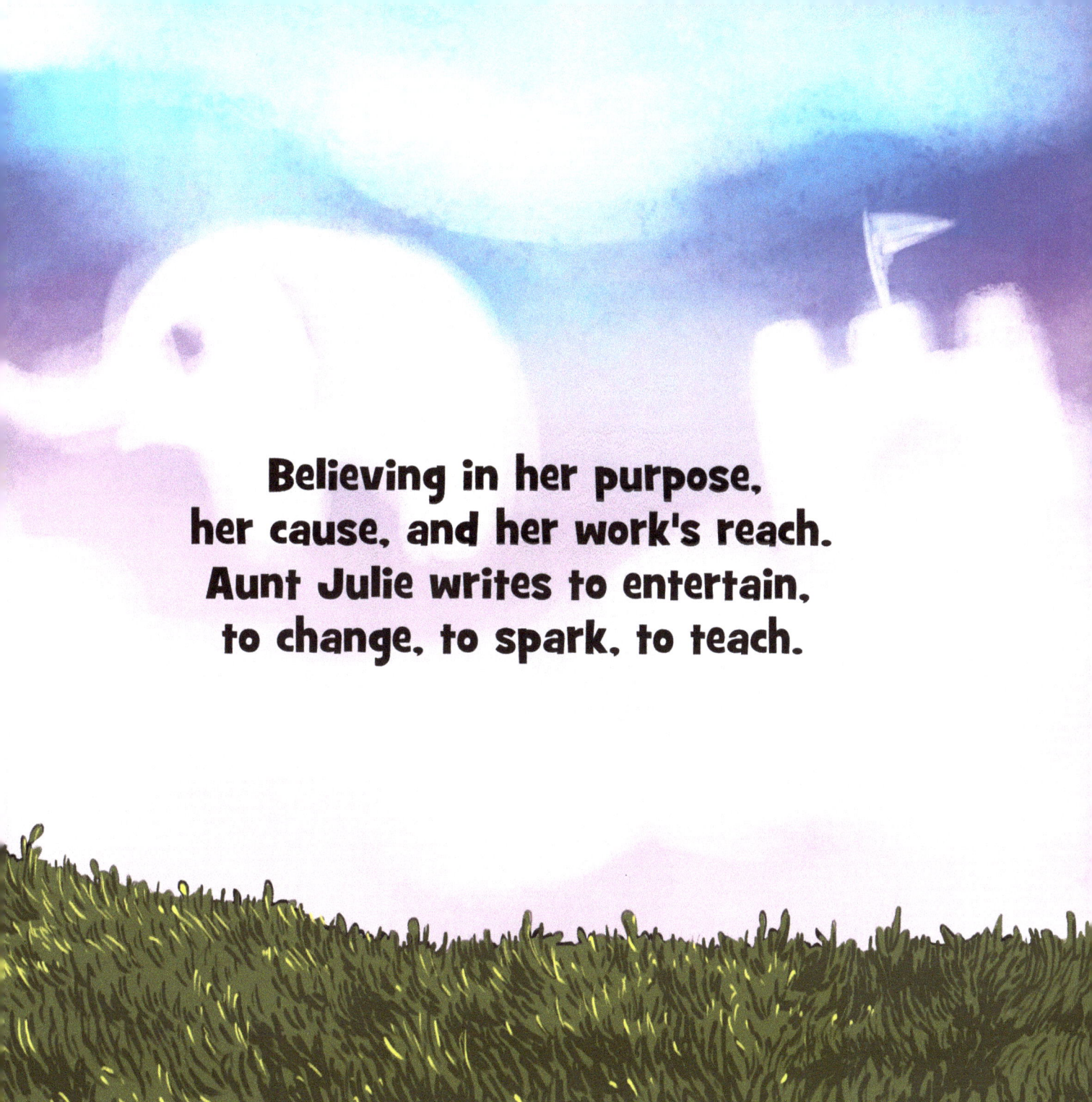

Each page filled with writing
causes a tickle or a laugh,
feelings or emotions
of sadness, grace, and love.

I'll be just like Aunt Julie,
when I'm big and fully grown.
Imagination turned to ink,
writing stories of my own...

...For writing is a power.
A true power to behold.
Impacting each reader.
Changing lives, young and old.

ABOUT THE AUTHOR

Writing under a number of pen names, Y. Eevi Jones is an award-winning & bestselling children's book author, and the founder of Children's Book University™. She was born in former East Germany to a German mother and a Vietnamese father. Thus, she spent an inordinate amount of her youth nosing through books that she shouldn't have been reading, and watching movies that she shouldn't have been watching. It was a good childhood.

Always drawing inspiration from her own two children, she loves to write about unique interests and aspires to find fun and exciting ways to have kids discover and learn about the magnificent marvels this world has to offer.

Eevi has been featured in Forbes, Scary Mommy, Huffington Post, Exceptional Parent Magazine, SCBWI, and more.

She can be found online at **www.BravingTheWorldBooks.com**.

A WORD BY THE AUTHOR

If you enjoyed this book, it would be wonderful if you could take a short minute to leave a lovely review on Amazon, as your kind feedback is very appreciated and so very important. It gives me, the author, encouragement for bad days when I want to take up scorpion petting. Thank you so very much for your time!

BRAVING THE WORLD™ SERIES

AWARD-WINNING SERIES

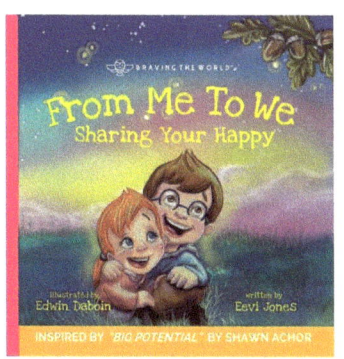
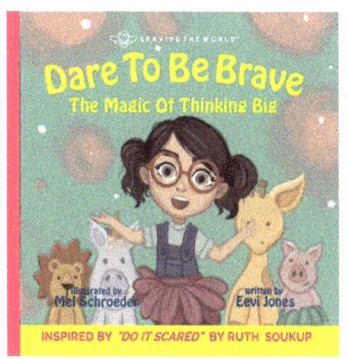
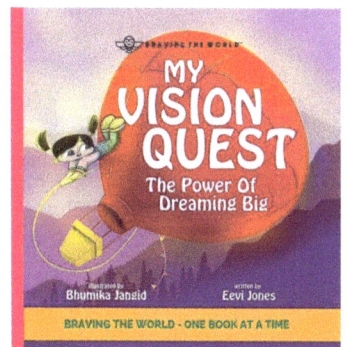

... AND MORE

OTHER WORKS BY THIS AUTHOR

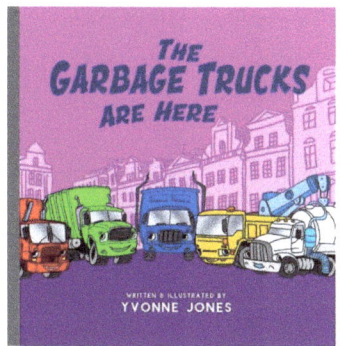

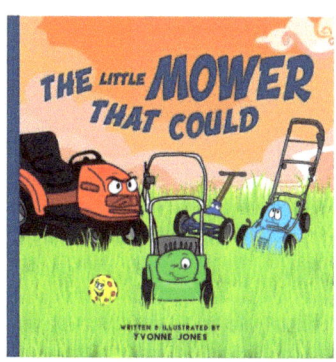
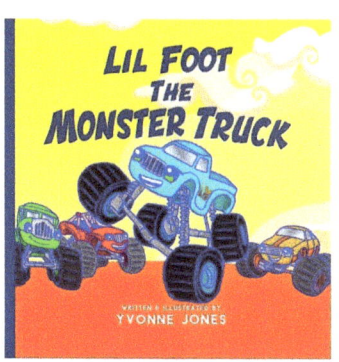
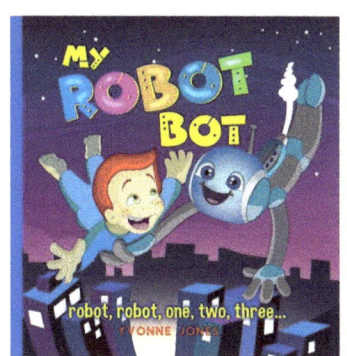
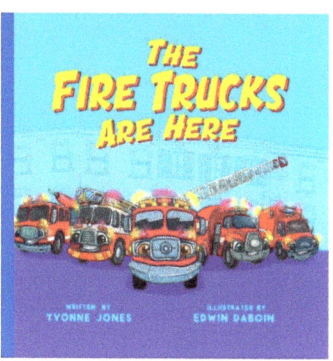

www.BravingTheWorldBooks.com

www.ingramcontent.com/pod-product-compliance
Lightning Source LLC
Chambersburg PA
CBHW041217240426
43661CB00012B/1070